INSCAPE
2017

WASHBURN UNIVERSITY
Department of English
1700 SW College Ave
Topeka, KS 66621

Thanks to the Washburn University Department of English.

There is another book that is the shadow
of my hand on this sunlit page, the one
I have tried hard to write, but let this do;
let gratitude redeem what lies undone.
~ Derek Walcott, 1930–2017

Vol. 42

inscapemagazine.org
washburn.edu/inscape
facebook.com/inscapemagazine

Cover Art: Detail from *Jazz Flavors,* by Linda Wimberly
acrylic, 20x20

Inscape, compiled annually at Washburn University in Topeka, Kansas, features poetry, fiction, nonfiction, and visual art from the region and beyond.

INSCAPE
2017

Contents

FICTION

Editors' Choice Award Winner:
8 INA ROY-FADERMAN *Bob and Dog*

28 JIM PLATH *For the Living*

56 SAVANNAH BROOKS *Smoke*

70 BARBARA BRADY *Misfits*

82 BARRY ZABELL *On Being Late*

NONFICTION

Editors' Choice Award Winner:
18 JULY WESTHALE *A Far Away Terrible Place*

42 PATRICIA FEENEY *Sunday Best*

66 ARIEL ALEXIA SULLIVAN *If People Were Rain...*

POETRY

Editors' Choice Award Winner:
14 COREY GINSBERG *On the Occasion of Watching an Adult Eat Pudding*

15 *A Broken Yolk*

36 ANNA MAXYMIW *The Strike*

37 FRANK RUBINO *Happy*

39 SUSANA H. CASE *Heart Like a Pine Cone*

40 MARTY CARLOCK *On Reading Billy Collins*

50 LAURA FAIRGRIEVE *Lovesong for the Moon Jellyfish*

52 *Mothing*

60 K.C. BRYCE FITZGERALD *Paradise Lost*

61 DEBORAH PHELPS *Blue Crabs*

62 SETH JANI *Dealer*

78 SUZANNE O'CONNELL *The Man in the Hat*

80 KENDRA TANACEA *Res Ipsa Loquitur*

81 DONNA EMERSON *I Never Wore a Training Bra*

86 PETER GRIMES *The Proposition*

ART

Editors' Choice Award Winner:
7 MARIA HAAG *Anthropomorphic Window*

17 *Concrete Jungle*

27 *Riven*

35 LINDA WIMBERLY *Jazz Flavors*

41 JAYNE MAREK *Sky Canal*

49 FABRICE POUSSIN *Winter*

55 KATHERYN LONG *Belger*

59 STEPHEN LINSTEADT *Weasel with Serpent Under Apuleius's Table*

65 *Yamdoot*

69 KEVIN ZEPPER *Garden Dragon*

77 KATHERYN LONG *Triangle Walks*

85 JASON HANNA *Smile While You Still Can*

EDITORS' CHOICE

ANTHROPOMORPHIC WINDOW
Maria Haag
acrylic on paper
13x9

BOB AND DOG

Ina Roy-Faderman

Bob and Dog's association began on a crisp and foggy Monday morning. Bob was six foot in his socks, with curly brown hair, running at a fair pace down the sidewalk in his blue running suit with white track stripes, hoping to finish his run before the 8 o'clock traffic started. Dog had a Labrador build, with short, reddish-brown fur, a pointer face, and a white muzzle. He had his nose to the ground, walking in a convoluted pattern in the opposite direction from Bob.

When Bob passed Dog, he asked, "What are you tracking?"

"Things," said Dog importantly, not lifting his nose. "Things."

*

Nonetheless, Dog consented to turn around and jog along with Bob. They stopped at the Lucky on the way home. There, Bob bought a blue collar and matching leash.

"Nice color," said Dog, when Bob emerged.

"Thank you," said Bob, trying not to sound proud. "I thought so."

When they got back to Bob's house, Bob called Jim, a co-worker. "I'm calling him Dog," said Bob. Jim, who always sounded enthusiastic, said, "I've always thought of you as a dog person. Great name, too."

"Thanks," said Bob. "I like it." They hung up, mutually content. Dog was sleeping near the fireplace, muzzle on his front paws.

*

Before Dog's arrival, Bob had had a routine. He got up at seven o'clock and went for a run. He came in, took a cool shower, and put on khaki shorts and a white shirt. He went to work—fixing computer hardware, nothing he was deeply interested in, but it paid the bills—stopped at the grocery store on the way home and bought food for dinner. On weekends, he and Jim would go to see a movie. Sometimes, Bob would spend Saturday evening at dinner with someone he'd met through Jim or work, and though they sometimes would have sex, they would never stay the night. He rarely saw the same woman twice; the women he met were superficial, and the constant fiddling with lipstick and nylons made him nervous.

Now, with Dog, things had changed. Bob had someone to talk to when he came home. Often Dog would tell him about the interesting day that he had had—squirrels he'd seen and cars that had passed by. In addition, Dog continued to enjoy tracking in his purposeful fashion during their early morning walks. One of Bob's new interests was trying to guess what it was that would walk in such a zig-zagging, erratic way. "Demons?" he suggested one day. This was one of the few topics on which Dog remained evasive.

"No," said Dog scornfully. "Only cats do that."

Despite his scorn, Dog had an on-going association with a tabby who lived next door and went by the name of Flash. Flash and Dog often sat or slept companionably in the sun. Flash's owner, a man named Jerry, commented on the oddity of this arrangement.

Later, Dog said, "That dog-cat stuff is all a myth anyhow."

*

Flash knew a lot of houses in the neighborhood, and thus Dog could tell Bob about the lives of various cat owners. Dog often told stories about these people as he lay at the foot of Bob's bed, before they fell asleep—a practice which Bob found soothing.

People stopped to talk to Bob during the morning run. Often they wanted to know what breed Dog was, and Bob would tell the story of their initial meeting in the chilly fog. These people would pat Dog, which Dog would submit to in regal though kindly silence. Bob sometimes asked Dog why he didn't talk to these other people, but Dog seemed to think the answer fairly obvious. To Bob, Dog offered thoughts about work, how to manage his boss, where to invest—in fact, the only information from his past which Dog offered to Bob was that at one time he had been owned briefly by an investment banker. When Bob asked him what happened to the banker, a man named Kelly, Dog said, "It was bound not to work," and then sighed, head on his paws.

Bob and Dog fell into a routine. After their morning walk, Bob went to work. When Bob got home, Dog would follow him around the house and they would have dinner together. At first, Bob resisted this practice. But when Bob didn't take the suggestion that they dine together seriously, Dog began carrying his dish to the table and eating at Bob's feet. The idea of Dog's jaws having to go through this exercise every evening filled Bob with much more dread than he might have expected. "What if it's damaging his teeth?" he thought as he watched Dog sitting near his feet. Finally Bob put the bowl on the table and pulled a chair near it, at the opposite end from where Bob always sat. Dog ate with impeccable manners, one front paw on each side of the bowl, never gulping and carefully wiping his muzzle on his napkin.

*

"What are you missing now from your life?" Dog said one night.

Bob considered this question while Dog sat with his head cocked, his left ear hanging limp. Before Dog had come into his life, he had had to jog alone. He had Jim to talk to, a job to go to, a radio to sing with. But now life was fuller. "Nothing," Bob said. He wanted to add, "now that I have you," but he felt somewhat shy and didn't.

"Wrong answer," said Dog, who then left the table without being excused—a first. He went to the fireplace, and lay down in his usual position—head on paws —but without closing his eyes. He appeared to be in deep thought. Bob watched him, puzzled, feeling the warmth of love expand briefly in his heart before calming back to a waiting ember. *What else could I want?* Bob thought.

*

The next day when Bob came home, Dog was sitting at the table. Sitting at one of the side chairs was a man facing Dog. Neither of them was talking. "Bob," said Dog, turning his muzzle toward him. *His eyes are twinkling,* thought Bob, realizing that he'd never seen Dog smiling before. "This is Jerry, from next door." Jerry turned to Bob, smiling, hand out. What a charming smile, thought Bob as their eyes met. "Please, stay for dinner," said Bob.

After dinner, Dog left to his place by the fireplace. Jerry asked Bob if he'd like to have a meal at a nearby Russian restaurant some time and Bob, to his own surprise, said yes, he would like that. In the corner of his eye, Bob could see Dog cocking his left ear and then lowering it again.

“I know what you’re up to,” Bob said to Dog that night.

*

After two dinners, a trip to the zoo, and two movies (one matinee and one midnight movie, at which Jerry and Bob agreed that Nicole Kidman couldn’t hold a candle to Katharine Hepburn), Jerry and Bob made love in Bob’s bed, in candlelight. Jerry had a surprisingly muscular body, which Bob could appreciate —tai chi, Jerry explained. Jerry in turn admired Bob’s lithe legs and his grace, and Bob explained, while Jerry rubbed his hand gently across Bob’s back, that he had at one time hoped to be a dancer. “Fiddling with wiring is okay though,” Bob said. When he finally realized that Dog wasn’t in the room, he padded out into the living room, wearing his shirt against the chill, afraid that Dog had felt shut out. But Dog was lying on the couch and looked up sleepily when Bob entered. “Can I come in now?” he said, and Bob felt anxious, wondering if this was an angry question.

“Of course,” said Bob, kneeling beside Dog. “You could have come in before.”

“On your first night?” Dog stretched his front paws out, a gesture that Bob suddenly recognized as belonging to Flash. “Don’t be silly.” Nonetheless, Dog padded after Bob back into the bedroom. Bob got back under the covers, and Dog went to his usual place at the foot of the bed. “I guess I should go,” said Jerry sleepily.

“Don’t go,” said Dog in his growly voice.

“Don’t go,” echoed Bob.

And so he didn’t.

*

After six months, Bob and Jerry tore down the fence between their houses and put a cat-flap into Bob’s back door. Bob and Jerry went to the grocery store every Saturday morning, leaving Dog tied to the bike rack to wait for them. Bob protested the leashing—after all, they knew he wouldn’t wander away—but Dog reminded them that it was the law. Early on, Bob asked Jerry whether Flash ever talked, and Jerry said, “Only to Dog, I guess.” He added, “What makes you so special anyhow?” but Dog just looked up at him and smiled back. Bob realized as he listened to Jerry’s matter-of-fact tone that he, Bob, had fallen in love.

Bob and Jerry celebrated Christmas in Jerry's house, because his bay window gave a beautiful view of the tree from the sidewalk, and Thanksgiving in Bob's. Bob met many of Jerry's friends, who came over for these holidays. Jim also came over, with his girlfriend Camellia, who was a better cook than any of the three of them. Bob had dreaded the first meeting between Jim and Jerry, but all Jim had said when Bob was getting him a beer was, "You sly dog, you. He's a good-looking guy." Jerry and Bob liked Thai better than Chinese, Magritte better than Matisse, and Macs better than PCs. They had some differences, though not over things that mattered—shoe size and the types of eggplant dishes they preferred. They both liked to decorate the Christmas tree the same way—with silvered glass, and clear ornaments, and little blue lights. "It's another sign," said Jerry when he opened up Bob's box of ornaments for the first time. They took turns jogging with Dog in the mornings since tai chi sometimes conflicted with the morning run. Jerry, whose workplace was a graphic design company, sometimes took Dog to work. Jerry's coworkers fed Dog treats and let him sit in any of the offices, so Dog enjoyed it, but since Flash spent the days that Dog was gone moping, Dog didn't consent to it very often.

*

Bob, Dog, Flash and Jerry were together for seven Christmases. On the evening of the eighth Christmas, Dog got up from the foot of the bed and nudged Bob gently with his wet nose. "Huh?" said Bob, whispering.

In the half-light from the street lamps, Bob could see Dog's white muzzle.

"It's time for me to go," said Dog.

"What do you mean?" Bob said, half-asleep.

"Don't worry, " said Dog, "I'll talk to you tomorrow."

In the morning, Bob and Jerry found Dog curled up under the Christmas tree, in his usual position, a peaceful expression on his face, eyes closed.

*

Later, Bob said, "I didn't know what he meant," sobbing in Jerry's arms.

*

Bob and Jerry stayed together eight more years. Flash died four years to the day after Dog, without ever having said a word to Bob. Bob and Jerry talked about finding other animals, but Jerry—unusual for him—seemed rather reluctant.

Bob, though with doubts, agreed. "It wouldn't be the same," he said to Jerry one night.

Jerry looked up, as if he'd been distracted. "No, I guess it wouldn't."

*

Two weeks later, Jerry told Bob about the cancer. Six months later, he asked to be home so that he could die in bed, the bed they'd first made love in. Bob stayed by his side all the minutes of the last two weeks, feeding him broth sometimes, and watching the body he loved get whittled away as if by a horribly blunt knife. Jerry's eyes, though, grew clearer and clearer, like ocean water with light behind it. In his sleep, he clutched his stomach and curled around it like a fetus. Often he would shiver as if the blankets were made of ice. Bob would curl around him, placing his arms carefully under the tubes, and say, "Does this help?" Jerry would nod, though the shivering didn't stop. *Dog would have told him stories,* Bob thought. So he told Jerry stories, about what it was like to learn ballet, about Flash, about the first time they met, and sometimes Jerry could smile and then fall asleep. One night before he fell asleep, Jerry said, "We have lots of love here." The next morning, Bob woke up, curled around Jerry's finally relaxed body, Jerry who was no longer clutching himself, his hands still surrounded by Bob's.

*

Often, Bob would wake up, and in the late night light, he would see shadows, outlines of Jerry at the table, Flash and Dog curled up side by side on the hearth. "Where are you?" he whispered once, and the shadows disappeared. After that, he didn't whisper again, but sat on the couch, watching as the ghostly grey figures went through the motions of day-to-day life—eating, drinking, laughing.

At work, co-workers began to tell Bob that he looked tired.

One morning, Bob woke up to find Dog by his bed, collar on and leash in his mouth. Bob looked at the walls dissolving around him. Jerry was nowhere to be seen, but he could sense him. "At the pub," said Dog before Bob could ask. "What took you so long?" Dog added.

Bob looked around again, at the sunshine streaming around him, and into Dog's kindly brown eyes. "I can't imagine," he said, as he took the leash into his hand and began to jog. "I can't imagine."

ON THE OCCASION OF WATCHING AN ADULT EAT PUDDING

Corey Ginsberg

Deplorable, this
submersion of tongue
into viscous,
chocolate wobble.
Spoon scraping sides—
greedy for
gelatinous blob.
Then: face plunging
into plastic mausoleum
for final quick lick.
Single-serving
demonstration
of desperation,
a reenactment
of a childhood
too soft to chew,
too substantial
to swallow whole.

A BROKEN YOLK

Corey Ginsberg

A broken yolk never forgets
how it felt to be intact, contained.
As it seeps onto the edges
of a greased pan and offers its essence
to a hungry brunchmonger,
it no longer has to choose
between appetite and expansion.

Editors' Choice

CONCRETE JUNGLE

Maria Haag

oil on canvas

24x36

A FAR AWAY TERRIBLE PLACE

July Westhale

February, 2013. Oakland, California.

"Read it to me," Francesca's voice comes through the line.

Unquestioningly, I begin:

"I remember being so young I thought all artists were famous."

"I remember being so young I thought all artists were good, kind, loving, exceptionally interesting, and exemplary human beings."

"There," she says, "That. I've just aged out of it."

*

Things Francesca and I Talk About Most (2011–present day)

The Fulbright, The Benjamin Saltman, the APR Honickman, Bread Loaf, Tin House, the NEA, the National Book Award, Sarabande, Norton, the Lammys, Astrea, the Ruth Lilly, the Yale Younger Poets, the Amy Lowell, Sewanee, Yaddo, Millay, Napa Valley, Tomales Bay, the grant from the Los Angeles Arts Commission, the Guggenheim. Who did I think was going to be teaching at Lambda this summer and had I kept up with Kevin's most recent book and had I seen who Eileen was shacked up with now and any word from Coleen about Eloise? What did I think about Saeed Jones' book, and when was the last time I'd heard from Major Jackson? Most importantly, what was the best new thing I'd read that just killed me?

Bob Hicok, I said. I always said him.

"You can't trust lesbians," she'd immediately recite.

When will you come visit please come visit if I give you my miles I've got lots how about now how about sooner there's this amazing exhibit dance party reading poet in town—

*

Read me *Dear Sugar.* Read me Eloise's poem about pulling the woman in through the window to fuck in the front seat. Read me Akhmatova. The poem about the flowers from a new love after a divorce. Nikky Finney's line about nipples. Anything by Naomi Shihab Nye. Read me the part where Katie Ford talks about people being so hot in Iran they sleep on their roofs. Would you sleep on a roof? What if it was a very tall roof, and no one could see you? What if everyone you loved was also on that roof? What if the roof was up a very slippery wall, and everyone you were afraid of was below and couldn't get you, and you could crank down a magical ladder for those you wanted to invite to join you? What if the roof was really the roof of the airport, and you could see all of the planes but they couldn't see you, and you didn't have to watch anyone cry at the Departures Gate? What if the roof had two of your very favorite things, but one of the things you feared most? Do you think they have trout in Iran?

*

2011.

Somewhere here, I moved to Salt Lake City.

It was an experiment in love. Call it an experiment in temperament. An experiment in martyrdom, isolation, sustainable urban gardening. It was an experiment in mortality, poetic integrity, and how long I could live without a decent burrito.

The scientific method asks the following:

Step one: ask a question.

Is this what you want? My partner and I are boxing our books, which collectively reach the hundreds, and our typewriters, which collectively reach the dozens, and our animals, which collectively outnumber us. We are selling our art supplies, our instruments, our summer clothes. *Our Bodies, Ourselves.* Surrounding us is the incessant, off-beat ticking of clocks, of which she (let's call her Charlie) has multitudes, and they, together, measure time without ceasing; which is to say, every second is thronged by another second of another clock which is beaten down by a stronger clock—and this is how we know where to place them in the house, by loudness of their voices, how much audio space they inhabit.

The day our acceptance letters came, for Ph.D. and M.F.A. respectively, we were driving full-speed through the Caldecott Tunnel, heading for higher ground. It was March 12th, 2011, the day after the tsunami in Japan, the debris from which still washes up on my Californian beaches, like lost pleas.

My Kia Rio was full of everything we'd determined was irreplaceable, since the 5 a.m. siren cut through Alameda, the makeshift island off Oakland, demanding that everyone head for Mt. Diablo. Among those in my backseat were the following: four cats, one Dalmatian, a safe full of money, two passports, our laptops, a picture of my mother, ten Larabars, two liters of water, an axe, a flashlight, kava tea, a sharps container, and extra tamoxifen, the chemo alternative Charlie shot into her thigh every day.

*

Charlie hesitates over the sharps box, almost full. It is nearing the end of summer. I am wrapping our already-chipped dishes in newsprint, careful not to get inky prints on them. The clock on the mantel scolds richly. We've decided to move to Utah, and everything in her body says she doesn't want to take cancer with us.

*

Step two: Do background research.

Many people have told me that their twenties were the best time of their lives. Facing the end of mine, I feel resentful and cheated by this. What they really should have said is this: Childhood is a place to learn how to understand the world in a realistic way. People are unhappy. They commit endless treacheries. They expect children to be adults. The end of

childhood means understanding adults to be children.

The beginning of your twenties is spent trying to have compassion for the child-adults, who were maybe only your age when they tried being adults for the first time.

Adolescence is like that old cartoon about Inside-Out Boy, a boy who has swung too hard over a swing set and flipped over it, turning himself entirely inside out. He is a mess of organs and bones, and a small red heart-shaped heart. You do not learn about anatomy from Inside-Out Boy. Instead, you realize you are exactly like him, with mismatched insides and non-consensual transparency. Whenever you have a thought or feeling, everyone knows about it. You try to build a wall, but the child-adults around you have special tools made specifically for dismembering. As you get older, you realize that hiding in a field of softness is actually the best way to hide all of your too-big, too-obvious feelings. The softest place near your house is a field of sunflowers. It'll do, until it's no longer the season for them. But by that time, you've met Inside-Out Girl.

The rest of your twenties, you suddenly turn into Sisyphus, only the boulder has spikes and glass. The boulder remembers everything you have broken, a composite ball of sharps that you must push up an indeterminable slope. The boulder remembers, as well, everything that has broken you, and thus you are pushing yourself up, too.

Step three: test your hypothesis by doing an experiment.

Kevin Young, "I am trying to break your heart":

> Loneliness is a science—
>
> consider the taxidermist's
> tender hands
>
> trying to keep from losing
> skin, the bobcat grin
>
> of the living.

We move to Utah during the hottest month, the animals panting in the backseat. The cross-eyed tom, the sweetest and dumbest of them, figures out how to unzip his carrier, and climbs into Charlie's lap as she drives.

From our move, this is a picture I have that remains. Charlie is wearing white cutoffs, her blonde hair blocking the sun but filtering it so that she looks like she's beginning to become part of the out-the-window-scape. Nevada, I think. The cat is orange and fat, one eye focused on either side of my head. He is leaning on the sharp part of her elbow. Both of them have expressions of resignation. Charlie is supporting him half-heartedly, with one long hand against his fur, and the other lazily on the wheel, as if it doesn't matter, the road. As if we could be driving anywhere, our lives an afterthought.

My letters to Francesca were my open forum, the place I took up space and sang the sad moon song of a girl monk, locked in a tower with the key in my non-dominant left hand. As it became clearer and clearer that Charlie was having an affair with a girl named Glory, I wrote:

I brought home two cases of wine from California, come have a bottle with me, sit in the slough of crickets & the horrible songs they sing.

*

2013. Oakland.

The year following my horrific breakup with Charlie, I kept the poem "Failing and Flying," by Jack Gilbert, taped to my bathroom wall.

Who could say the marriage failed?

Suicidal but mostly mortified, I moved back to California. I rented a little studio that was shaped like a coffin. I contemplated dropping out of school, but was coaxed into staying, like a cat on the ledge of a thirtieth-story balcony. People came by and fed me and helped me unpack. When forced to cook for myself, I made smoothies—so many smoothies. Smoothies with protein powder, smoothies with foraged fruit. Smoothies made of kale about to go bad from neglect, and smoothies made from ice and grapes. So many smoothies that I forgot what food looked like when it wasn't masticated. I spent days and days prostrate on the floor of my therapist's office, muffling the words "what if this is the one thing I can't recover from?"

I pictured Charlie and Glory wearing matching t-shirts that screamed UTAH UTAH UTAH. Imagining they were doing everything Utahn one could do: picking apples, going to church, saying golly, wearing visors.

My therapist would soothe: *theses are the stories you tell yourself.*

My therapist said, "Sweet one. This is what recovery looks like."

"Recovery can eat a bag of dicks," I muffled.

"Yes, it can," she cooed, sympathetically.

Winter was a long stretch of moving from body to body, trying to inhabit someone else, some body; not mine. Not my body, a big, open sky of a wound, a sunset of my guts. The kindness of others searing me through.

If it were a good day, I'd ask myself triumphantly, who could say the marriage failed?, an upbeat to my chin. On days where I was lucky to make it to the mirror, I'd stare at the last line—the one about Icarus coming to the end of his triumph.

"I could see her in the water, when love was fading from her." The phone was tucked in my hair, held to my face by a stuffed bear.

"Oh, Jukebox," Francesca is sighing from Michigan. "There is no way to trace that fade."

2013 was a year when Francesca and I were both so broke, a bag of clementines was like buying us the sun. If we could scrape together the airline miles, she'd come to my studio in North Oakland—the Coffin—and I'd turn off all the lights and switch on my five-dollar star machine. The machine had four sounds, and all of them were horrible. The worst was one that sounded like a heartbeat. I would turn the heart up as loud as it could go, recite *"the night the stars burned so bright everyone knew they'd never last."* The sound of fake blood pumping was loud and violent, the room gash-red and pulsating.

"I want to leave Michigan," she said, looking at the garish red stars spinning on my ceiling. An ex-lover had made a pedestal for the star machine that had a disco ball motor, so it spun as lazily as a middle school slow song. "I feel very much like Theodore Roethke, married to the place."

"You'd rather be Richard Hugo," I chided, gently. I realized she hasn't read *Triggering Town* and I gave her my worn-through copy. I gave her *The Room Where I Was Born, Head Off & Split, White Egrets.*

*

Born and raised on a trout farm in Northern Michigan, for Francesca being queer was largely a private, sheltered thing—or something to be shouted in the canyons small urban communities made. Once, while she was visiting New York, she wrote to me about the magical disorientation of being in a place where women were openly gay: *Every time I see women holding hands I think oh Gd: 'have you too, come here from a far away terrible place? Probably. I love you.'*

Me: *"Have you ever felt desperate in a far away terrible place? I wish I could call you to come over, go on the swings with me, take walks in the giant alleys behind the houses here and duck through the sunflower caves. I have been planting things when I feel such desperation for common ground—planting bulbs & bulbs that will come up late spring as blues, yellows. Padding the window seat in the living room so that, six months from now, I'll be able to see what's come out of the gut of these giant seeds, knowing that there is life in some future way."*

Paisley Rekdal, from "Happiness":

> If I could not have made this garden beautiful
>
> I wouldn't understand your suffering,
>
> nor care for each the same, inflamed way.
>
> I would have to stay only like the bees,
>
> beyond consciousness, beyond
>
> self-reproach, fingers dug down hard
>
> into stone, and growing nothing.

*

August, 2011. Salt Lake City, Utah.

When I am not meeting Francesca in Michigan, or Savannah, or Los Angeles, or Oakland, or Chicago, or Boston, or once even Ohio at 3 a.m. after I disembarked my Greyhound bus too early, half-awake—when I'm not flying to meet her, then I am having persistent conversations about trauma.

"I just think that women are pigeon-holed into writing about feelings and shit," I say to Charlie, who is eating Morning Star vegetarian chicken nuggets with romaine right over the kitchen sink. This is her staple meal, though sometimes she'll branch out and eat baby carrots with hummus, or an entire pound of M&Ms. I admire the deftness of her microwave skills, how she pulls the nuggets out at the perfect moment before they become chewy. How she eats them slowly, instead of diving into them, a habit so different from my own constant starvation. I would eat the whole box, and if the situation were dire enough, I would eat the box, too.

I am indiscriminately insatiable—I would just as quickly eat food from the floor as devour an entire section of a library. I frequently fall into the many rabbit-holes of the Internet. I am known to sleep with people on the first date, in the bathroom or the car, sometimes intentionally forgetting underwear, or to wear silk stockings that lead a trail right up the backs of my thighs. Charlie's ability to move slowly in the world is beyond my scope of understanding, but within my realm of admiration.

She gums at her soy nugget like a koala eating a eucalyptus leaf, her shoulders slightly rigid. I correct myself quickly, because I don't mean to say that I have ill will towards feelings. In truth, I am beginning to love feelings. It's a new thing for me.

"And many women do, or many people socialized as female," I add. "And it's important to do so—there's a very radical component to writing about feelings, especially for us. I think this is in large part due to living a life in the margins, where all feelings are considered some large landscape of a country called Hysteria, where all women live."

The thought of Hysteria as a country suddenly makes me burst out laughing, the water glass in my hand slipping onto the floor and splitting so cleanly, it looks purposeful. The cracked glass seams a wide grin, and I feel a sense of camaraderie. In Hysteria, women likely break glasses every day. Because the women of Hysteria are born from a place where they're no longer dissociated from everything they've been through, and they are allowed the entire gamut of expression.

I once read a book my therapist recommended to me that said animals don't experience PTSD. When something happens to them—a tiger stalking after them and they narrowly escape, a hunter's bullet grazing their haunches—they find a dark place to shake and shake. The shaking is the body's natural way of working out something terrible, so it doesn't instead find a dark place inside of you to hide and stay.

I imagine that Hysteria has catacombs for women to shake in, for as long as they need.

When I feel the cold shock of water reaching my big toe, I realize that Charlie has stopped eating her dinner completely, and is staring at the glass. It is a favorite of hers. The dog has somehow nudged open the baby gate that separates the kitchen from the living room and, sensing Charlie's distress, immediately begins puking into the water. Within seconds, I am on my knees, sopping up the muddy stream of vomit, entirely forgetting about the glass until I see that the water has turned a kind of dusty rose. I feel repulsed by the dog's insides, until I stand and feel my left knee buckle under me, a large shard worked into the meat of my knee.

I am still laughing about Hysteria, so hard that my mouth has only the shape of laughter—there are no sounds. Charlie is rolling down my patterned tights, ripping the fabric around the knees, right through a silver moon. Her mouth is set, though covered in light brown crumbs, and it is never so clear to me that she is a nurse's daughter. Fixing her hands on either side of my knee—where is her Morning Star?—she deftly plucks the glass from below the bone as if she were pulling up a fennel bulb, using another hand to catch the blood.

I am suddenly gelatinous, flopped over like a Fortune Telling Fish. My arms splay to the West, my torso sinking to the floor as if my spine were tied to an anchor thrown to the middle of the Earth.

"Sometimes I imagine my tailbone is tied to an anchor thrown to the middle of the Earth." Francesca? My therapist? The woman at the queer free clinic who prescribes me Xanax? "And in this way, I feel grounded."

Charlie is examining the red glass to measure for thickness, depth. In my sudden bonelessness, I can see she is also sadly noting the break in the glass's bright tulip pattern, cut clean from the stem. My blood is hidden safely under the pressure of her hand. She looks from the glass, to my knee, to my face, which has sunken to the Earth's molten core.

"How did you not feel that?" she asks.

Editors' Choice

RIVEN
Maria Haag
oil on canvas
36x24

FOR THE LIVING

Jim Plath

I wondered if all funeral homes looked like that one. On the outside, humble bricks and mortar, easy to miss, like a blemish on a face you've seen too much of to stop and look at it. On the inside, everything lacquer and polish, sterile, impermeable, as if any surface could be wiped clean with a paper towel. If you were the type that believed in spiritual energies, I supposed you'd want that. That kind of place holds so much grief, and rarely anything else, you'd want to build it out of things that washed easily. In the corner, a marble column reflected the pulsing glow of the fireplace beside an open door and a sign that bore a dead woman's name.

I didn't know the woman, though I'd met her twice. She'd thought our second meeting was our first, and I didn't correct her. Some people relish an opportunity to play the wounded party. They collect apologies like firewood, but I've never been one of them. This woman and I were two strangers who once passed close enough to one another that not speaking would have been awkward. That was the extent of it.

My wife worked with her. They were in their company's payroll department. Judging from what I've been told, that meant sharing a break room refrigerator, covering each other's extensions on lunch breaks, and nodding in the elevator. There may have been more to it, but it didn't matter. Her co-workers expected my wife to show up, and that's why I was there, dressed like a chauffeur, nodding at strangers who roved the lobby like school children waiting on a bell.

The viewing room held more chairs than people. A small portrait hung on display before the open casket. Inside, the woman's skin appeared to have lost as much color as her hair, and in her off-white dress, she looked like something carved from limestone.

From speakers above the entryway, violins played something soft and slow, a generic melody, but with the rising, labored pitch of something crying out before it broke. These types of sounds meant to convey an innate sadness, something that could be understood without being explained, the way that blood-red paint expressed urgency. The whimper of a violin could show sadness, or create it. This served to remind people like me—whose spouses or work obligations brought them—that they were among the bereaved.

My wife took my hand and squeezed it, stroked my index finger with her thumb and gave some fraction of a smile. She always knew how to do that: how to find space between subtle and coy, then make a home of it. "We won't have to stay too long. Just let me go and find some people."

I nodded and she wandered off.

The good thing about someone dragging you to a funeral is you don't really have to hide it. Nobody's supposed to be happy to be there. Nobody's supposed to be happy at all, and in that, I found another type of person: the type who wore grief like a spotlight. These were the types of people who still went on about how their neighbor's cousin's barber's college roommate knew someone who almost died in the towers on 9/11. They always knew someone battling cancer, or a family whose house burned down at Thanksgiving. For those people, every tragedy was an opportunity to grab some piece of local fame. That's never been me either, and I'm glad for that. I've always thought it must be exhausting to live that way.

If anything, I knew my wife had the harder role to play. I got to be the disinterested stranger. If I needed to address anyone at all, I could offer some platitude wrapped in condolences, lower my head and move on. My wife had no such luxury. She worked in a small office. Everyone played politics. It didn't matter if a co-worker worked only part time, or if no one in the office knew them well. Not showing up at their funeral would be perceived as a statement, but it wasn't enough to just show up. She'd need to look unsettled without seeming to upstage close friends and family. I became convinced that some mathematical formula existed for navigating these types of social situations, and I never cared to learn it. In moments like that, I basked in an abiding gratitude for my tiny home-office, and the precarious life of the self-employed man.

Being in that room felt like the world's longest elevator ride. You knew other people were there, but you didn't want to engage. You never knew where you should be looking, so you tried not to let your eyes settle on any one location for too long. All you could hope for was that it'd be over soon, and you'd be gone before things got too cramped.

Wandering around the room, I wanted to find somewhere to pass the time. No place felt right to sit. If I sat too close to the casket, I felt like an imposter; too far away, and I felt like a voyeur. I took a seat halfway back in the aisle behind a man with thinning brown hair. He wore a black t-shirt, a week's worth of stubble, and a stale musk, like an old dirt floor.

He turned partway around and looked me over. "Do I know you?"

I started to answer, but I felt my throat dry out. I paused, took a breath, and tried again. "I don't think so. My wife worked with," I bobbed my head toward the front of the room. I couldn't recall the dead woman's name, not from meeting her, or from the sign outside the viewing room.

The man chuckled. His breath stank of onions and stale beer. "Figured you were here for my dad."

I wondered why he'd assume that, but didn't want to ask any questions. "Sorry. I'm just here for my wife."

He faced forward and muttered, "Enjoy the show."

When I was maybe ten, and had to go to services for a great-grandfather I'd never met, I complained. My mom scolded me, told me funerals weren't really about the person who'd died, but the people they left behind. Mom said funerals were for the living.

I wanted to apply that reasoning again. Maybe if I felt I knew someone who grieved for the old woman, I'd feel like I had someone who really needed me there. Then I could feel better about loitering near a stranger's corpse.

On first glance, my prospects were not encouraging. Across the aisle from me, a young blonde woman studied her face in the screen of her smartphone. She adjusted the underwire of her bra and the neckline of her dress and snapped a picture. I didn't think she needed consolation.

When my wife came back, she wore a strange expression, like her face froze before she could grimace. She leaned in and murmured, "We may have to hang around. They're asking some of us to say a few words."

"Doesn't a priest or a family member usually do that?"

Her eyes widened. "I guess, but they're the ones asking."

I nodded, and she wandered off to work out what she and the other coworkers would say.

I thought more about my great-grandfather's funeral. I remembered the wreath and bouquets that shrouded his casket, the crowded church, and a man giving a long eulogy in a voice that shook and cracked as though it could only escape his lips in sporadic bursts.

In my early teen years, I fantasized about running away from home. When my parents grounded me for skipping school or sneaking out after curfew, I imagined punishing them by spending a night in the woods or on a park bench. What if a car hit me as I walked across the freeway in the middle of the night? Would they get to the hospital before my organs gave out? Maybe they'd get there just in time to say they were sorry, or at least admit they were wrong. Or else, maybe I'd just have to watch them cry as a specter floating above my own body. I wondered if my funeral would be anything close to what my great-grandfather's was, or if it took a full lifetime to earn that sort of sendoff. I think only a child could be so facetious as to wonder about these things.

More people trickled into the viewing room. A pair of young men whispered to one another as they stepped through the doorway. I couldn't hear what they said, but they each stifled a laugh over it. After them, a middle-aged man took a pull from a flask and wiped his mouth on his shirt sleeve. I abandoned the sort of egocentric fantasies about my own funeral once my pubescent hormones quieted, and I became distracted with learning to drive and unhook a bra, but in that moment, I couldn't help but hope that whatever my funeral looked like, I would be better represented than this.

Empty chairs still outnumbered people, but the room felt full. I suppose it was sort of in the way a lone fly floating in your drink makes your cup seem full of bugs. I got up, shuffled past a man in plaid playing solitaire on his tablet, and headed outside for some fresh air.

Away from the door, a young woman in a black pantsuit leaned against a brick column and lit a cigarette. She nodded and asked, "Do you know if Martin's here yet?"

"Martin?"

She nodded. "Gloria's husband."

I remembered the sign then. That was the dead woman's name. "Right, the—"

"Woman whose funeral this is?"

"Sorry," I said through my teeth.

She shrugged. "Sorry for what? You're showered and dressed. I figured you had to be here for Martin."

"I never met him. I'm here with my wife. She used to work with Gloria."

She took a drag off her cigarette. "You left her alone in there, did you?"

"They're asking her and some of her coworkers to say a few words, I guess."

She dipped her head forward and snickered. "Are you serious?"

I couldn't tell if she was more surprised or amused. I didn't answer her.

Her lips pulled again at the filter. When she exhaled, she pursed her lips, turned her head from side to side and watched the thin trail of smoke, spreading and closing like a veil around her face. She stared at the stem of rolled paper turning to ash between her fingers. "Whenever these things kill me, I really hope they don't just get my coworkers to speak at my funeral."

Though seconds earlier, I'd thought the same thing, I searched for something else to say, but I had nothing to add, or at least nothing that I really wanted to add. "So, how do you know the family?"

"Small town. Everybody knows everybody."

"You're close to her husband, though?"

She nodded. "Well, I guess so. He was my math teacher in high school. My senior year, I got rear-ended at a light, messed my back up. He came to the house himself to tutor me. I don't think I'd have graduated on time without him."

"Must have meant a lot to you."

She pointed toward the door. "Not just me. Look around in there. All those people, or at least the ones who look like they bathe? They came for Martin."

"I wonder why he's not here yet."

The woman dropped her cigarette and pressed it under her heel. "Someone's probably bringing him. I think he's in assisted living."

"I think I ran into his son earlier. He was sitting in front of me."

"Won't be his son bringing him. That'd be too decent of him."

She went back inside, but I lingered to enjoy the company of brick columns and a pair of ground squirrels running like streaks of rain across the funeral home's manicured lawn. I'd come there that day telling myself I didn't know the woman in the casket. Whatever part of me held fast to the idea of not speaking ill of the dead still wanted to believe I didn't know her. My mom once told me you can tell a person's character by the company they keep, but dead people have no say in who comes to bury them. Then I thought more about funerals being for the benefit of the living. The dead woman—Gloria—had a husband. Her husband was well-loved enough to draw a crowd, and he must have loved her.

Back in the viewing room, the music stopped. There were still plenty of open seats, but I chose to stand at the back of the room. Over by the casket, a young, red-haired woman asked for the crowd's attention. Her features were dulled in the room's soft light, and her voice wavered. From where I stood, I couldn't hear whatever anecdote she told. I could only discern that she was, in fact, speaking.

Through the open door behind me, I heard staggered footsteps and soft voices approaching from the lobby. An old man stepped into the viewing room. He was bald, but for some long wisps of white hair in a horseshoe around his head. His skin looked like cracked papier-mâché with pools of dark purple along the backs of his hands. He wore a suit that looked as though it had been draped over him.

To the old man's left, a man, pot-bellied with a dark-gray goatee, lagged behind. He was younger, but still too old to have been his son. I assumed this was some friend of the old man, and that the old man himself was Martin. The younger man wore a dark suit which was clean and pressed. His hair—though thin—was combed and washed, and he moved with the care and rigidity of an honor guard.

From a seat across the aisle from me, a young man, early in his twenties, rose.

He waved his hand across his body. "Hi, Grandpa."

The old man looked up, but began to lose his footing.

His escort rushed to his side. "It's okay, just get to a seat. You can say hello later."

Martin recovered, though his gaze fell on the front of the room, to the open casket that displayed his wife's body. He stopped, though his legs wobbled under him. His escort placed a hand under his arm.

The red-haired lady stopped her eulogy to allow the newcomers to find their place. Martin and his son inched forward. They were within arm's reach of me when they paused again. Martin's lips curled into a frown, and his dark brown eyes combed the room. He leaned in toward the goateed man who reached out to support him at the elbows. In a breathy voice, Martin asked, "Who died?"

His escort's gaze dropped, and he stroked Martin's arm. "It's Gloria."

Martin's brow flexed, and he bobbed his head. "I'm sorry to hear that." He wiped the corners of his mouth. "I used to know a Gloria."

JAZZ FLAVORS
Linda Wimberly
acrylic
20x20

THE STRIKE

Anna Maxymiw

Dave says it's *a strike against me.* At this fishing lodge forty miles south of James Bay, the name of my city is just another plate of pancakes on my forearms, another chore this housekeeper has to learn. So I work harder. I learn to weave between cooks and servers. Across the wet boat rails, among the rain-sleek backs of dockhands, I stay quiet. I don't ask why.

Dave doesn't say anything else about it. I watch him balance on his gunwales as he stares hard at the water, ordering me around, elbow-deep in his tackle box. But I get it. I see. Toronto—its subway lines hard like iliac crests, its parks cradling boozy couples like diamante in muskeg, its people who don't know Dave the hunter, the fisherman, the curious, the nasty, he who crouches beside me, contracts glottis and gnarls the flying geese out of flock-tight arrows, he who knows every curve of this blood-coloured lake—scares the shit out of him.

HAPPY

Frank Rubino

Die happy but die and so happiness ends.
Death's escapee seemed to pop through the back of a moving bus—

racing the light on 34th, he was almost run over,

emerged in the crosswalk and grinned ladies and gentlemen great to be here.
Lamb kids are born excited like him,
stand up amazed, soon they jump back and forth
shaking out their new muscles. People
aren't meant to be children
their whole lives,

though they want to be when old songs play in grandma's kitchen.

I'm in grandma's apartment in Wallington
on that street where food,
warm and sour, first made my glucose,

my brain memories.
I'm in a school auditorium.
A stage that smells like varnish, sweat and feet.
The girl one riser down,
her smaller body in her corduroy

jumper with wide straps, egg-yellow buttons—

close-up she smells like shampoo.

Scrape the dark off the middle, the pane clears.
Even through scratches
you see her, that quiet where you want to
be without doing.

HEART LIKE A PINE CONE

Susana H. Case

After your heart attack, I got into my car,
drove through Pennsylvania,
until a broken gas feed stopped me.
I had tried to outrun death.
Hunting season, men and guns among the trees.
Everywhere, there were glassy-eyed deer
strapped to cars. I regretted that I fled,
but later is always too late. I slipped back
to your semi-attached home, said I loved you,

mouthed the names on your new pill bottles,
promised I'd research them later.
The heart sits in a protective sac, and I built
my pericardium surround instead of Aphrodite's
magic sash. Slowly, spark
darkened. I took to reading late at night,
mystery books that bored me.

I made fancy meals for your friends,
schooled myself on sauces and organ meats,
all burners lit. Have you ever simmered heart?
How tough the meat is—
some say the heart is shaped like a pine cone,
its woody scales open only in heat.

ON READING BILLY COLLINS

Marty Carlock

Yes but Billy I saw same as you
mullions making a Hopper painting on the wall
wine and sun turning an enamel tabletop to stained glass

the ordinary day passing unremarked
so valuable all the same

The difference is you sit smug at your window
with your sharp pencil and your notebook that can become a bird
knowing your thoughts will end in my hand
their verticals and serifs ordered
like a row of carrot tops in the garden

You will never read mine
which lie dogeared on my desk, tea-stained
a grocery list written on the back.

SKY CANAL
Jayne Marek
photography
11x8

SUNDAY BEST

Patricia Feeney

I first saw an African-American in the flesh on Easter Sunday in 1960. I was eight years old, driving with my family through Forest Park in St. Louis. Until then, my interracial experience was limited to *The Little Rascals*: Buckwheat and Cotton, their hair electrified in disarray, their skin the deep, rich shade of day-old Folger's coffee, and their scripted hilarity drawn from the racial stereotypes of the times. More than 50 years later I can picture Buckwheat rubbing a genie's lamp and intoning his dreams: "I wish Cotton was a monkey," "I wish I had a watermelon."

I spotted the black girl from the window of our new Mercury station wagon. She appeared to be about my age, and like me, was with a large family. She skipped behind her parents and a collection of children, who, if lined up by size, would mirror the staircase of siblings that inhabited my home. My family of nine moved slowly through the log-jammed traffic, seeking a parking spot near the Zoo. Her family meandered in the opposite direction in small groups of twos and threes, laughing and calling out to one another. Her parents' arms were linked.

Two months earlier, four Negro college students staged a peaceful sit-in at a Woolworth lunch counter in Greensboro, North Carolina. This event, which was reprised over the following days, drew hundreds of Negro students to the Woolworth store, and became a template for future civil rights demonstrations that spread across the country. As our red station wagon inched through the Park, I knew nothing of this quickening movement. While I sat silently sandwiched between my siblings, a rip tide of revolt roiled beneath the surface of our lives.

"Jesus Christ, we're never going to find a spot," my father muttered. He wore his suit from church, a white starched collar peeking from the top of his dark suit jacket. We all were dressed in our Easter clothes. From the middle seat,

I watched the back of my parents' necks, my father's muscles tightening, my mother's relaxed.

"Try down by the Muny," my mother answered. "It's such a nice day we can walk." She held the baby on her lap. I sat between a sister and a brother; three more brothers occupied the last seat, which faced backward, the coveted caboose of our family train.

"If I could get over to the Muny, I would," my father's voice was low, his words clipped. "But we're not moving. I think we'll be here for the rest of the goddamned day."

"There's a cop ahead directing traffic. We'll move," my mother responded. She always spoke to him without fear. I never understood that.

Stuck in a line of traffic on that warm April day, only my parents spoke freely. The brothers in the caboose pushed and picked at each other, but their whispered protests didn't reach the ears of our parents. None of us wanted our father to hear us.

Leaning forward to look out the window, I watched the little girl circle her parents as they paused, looking about. Though I didn't hear their words, I imagined what they were saying: *Should we picnic here? Do you want to find a place with more shade?*

*

"Beautiful," my father growled when the baby began to whimper. My mother removed the baby's lacy hat and bounced her into a temporary silence.

My father's mood edged from contained impatience to open disgust. He was surrounded by his children, held captive in close quarters in the station wagon, no escape at hand, no parking space to leave the car, and no beer to smooth the edges of the wife-enforced family outing. He banged his fist on the steering wheel.

I ran my white-gloved hands over the folds of my Easter dress, caressing the stiff fabric of my store-purchased dress, a rare departure from my cousins' hand-me-downs. I felt at home in this expanse of yellow and white block checks, a generously gathered skirt that fell from a cinched belt that buckled in the front. A little jacket topped the dress. Made from the same yellow and white fabric, the jacket had a white linen and lace collar and white cuffs that fell just below my elbows. My mother called them "three-quarter-length sleeves." The way she said it made me feel grown-up. She curled my hair the night before and shaped it beneath a stiff, white hat the next morning before church. As I sat in our station wagon, I recalled the touch of her hands, reliving the moment I saw myself in the mirror before we left for church. I struggled to focus on that moment as I gazed at the girl with the skin I'd never seen "in real life."

In 1960 they were called Negroes if you used the refined term, or Coloreds if you were unaware there *was* a refined term and were acting civilly. If you were willfully bigoted, you used words that were unspeakable in my father's presence. My paternal grandmother was the only person who openly defied my father's position on the Negro race. She didn't restrict her language to acceptable terms. She used the N-word liberally. I spent enough time with her to connect this malicious word with Negroes, though it seemed as if she were referring to an imaginary nation, people I heard about and watched on television, but never saw in real life. My father railed against my grandmother's attitude. He told my mother it was a good thing there were Negroes, so his mother had someone to look down on.

"She finally found someone lower than the Irish," he declared one evening after an exhaustive critique of her prejudice.

*

The Civil Rights Act passed four years after my family's visit to Forest Park. The National Voting Rights Act passed a year after that. In 2014, 54 years after that Easter drive, 18-year-old Michael Brown was fatally shot by a police officer 10 minutes from my childhood home. Witnesses stood by contradictory accounts of the shooting. Some claimed Michael Brown was murdered as he stood with his hands up in surrender; others claimed the officer defended himself as Michael Brown rushed toward him. Ferguson, Missouri, erupted into weeks of protests, culminating in November when a grand jury declined to indict the police officer. Looters ransacked businesses and set buildings on fire, leaving the community smoldering.

Driving through Ferguson, a hotbed of shopping and restaurants during my childhood, I stared at a burned carcass of a city. In an attempt to heal the community, local artists painted multi-colored graffiti over the scars: peace signs and flowers adorned plywood that covered the remains of businesses. The police presence ebbed and flowed in Ferguson, corresponding to a scathing Justice Department analysis of policing in Ferguson, resignations of City officials, and the non-fatal shootings of two Ferguson police officers.

My father's 1960s defense of Negroes pitted him against his mother and fueled his outrage against the social policy of the day. Years later I learned of his work on behalf of black workers, using his executive position in manufacturing to hire those no one would touch.

One day my father's zeal for the oppressed spilled out on my oldest brother, Billy. My father lifted the back of his shirt and the waist of his khaki pants and threw him against the hall wall.

"Don't ever say that word!" my father said with a half-hearted kick to Billy's side as he lay in a heap, surprise and pain on his face.

Later I whispered to the second brother: "What word?"

"Nigger," he said, barely breathing.

Billy never again used this word when our father was present, but I'm certain he used it. A budding stand-up comic with a mean streak, he entertained our mother, an adoring audience. Billy was a skilled mimic, adept at characterizing stereotypes of the vulnerable: "retarded" school children, "lard-ass" girls, cripples, and Negroes. During such performances, Billy referred to Negroes as "Nigs." Perhaps my mother found this term a reasonable compromise. She covered her mouth when Billy performed the stereotype of a slow-witted Negro, but her eyes betrayed her smile. I didn't understand how my mother could be unaware of the danger in Billy's brand of humor. I loved my mother and wanted to be in league with her, but I was scared to trigger my father's wrath.

*

As the Forest Park traffic inched forward, the Negro girl spun in a circle, the yellow and white block-checked skirt of her dress lifting slightly with the breeze as she wrapped her three-quarter-length sleeves across the front of her matching jacket. Pulling away, I saw her smile up at her parents, hugging her new dress. I took off my gloves and rubbed the fabric of my—*our*—dress between my fingers. It scratched against my cuticles.

I felt tears gather in my sinuses. I wanted my mother's attention. *Look! Look at her, Mom. Look at that girl.* But I was afraid to speak. In 1960 I didn't know about the explosive Civil Rights movement, but I understood directing attention to the family with the dark skin could ignite an explosive reaction in *my* family.

I didn't want my father to hear, for fear he would fault me for calling attention to our identical dresses.

And why shouldn't she be in the same dress? Doesn't she deserve an Easter dress?

I didn't want Billy to hear for fear he would use the Negro girl to ridicule me when my father was out of earshot.

You and your Nig friend been shopping lately?

*

On the day of my family's 1960 Easter drive, no one could have predicted the 2014 events in Ferguson or the police shootings of black men across the country that followed. Each death after Michael Brown's triggered a public outcry, a trend many call the "Ferguson effect." Meetings, conferences, and "dialogues" to address institutional racism spread across the country like kudzu. Nearly two years after Michael Brown's death, the rhetoric and gunfire escalated. Police killings of black men continued while officers in Dallas and Baton Rouge were ambushed and murdered.

In the wake of the Michael Brown shooting, I attended a "Sacred Conversation on Race," sponsored by a handful of St. Louis churches. The discussion was led by a white man, who was assisted by two women, one white and one black. I scanned the room, which held 50 or 60 people, all white participants except for two, one who exited after the first half hour. I was dismayed and wondered how a group of mostly white people would have a conversation on race, sacred or otherwise.

The discussion leader wore us down over the course of the event, pressing us to confess our micro-aggressions: the many unconscious ways we assert white privilege. The group leader told us white people are not aware of the depth of our assumed privilege, which takes many forms, including well-meaning, but demeaning views of people of color. An 80-year-old white woman was chastised for taking pride in living in a majority-black neighborhood. Her pride was deemed a micro-aggression. A middle-aged white man broke down in tears for his "racist behavior," which we were left to imagine.

As the evening drew to a close, I shrank with embarrassment as I listened to white people congratulate themselves on their color-blind experiences, perhaps in response to the shame in the air.

"When I was a kid, my family swam in a hotel pool that only black people used. I remember playing with the black kids. We had a ball."

"I raised my son to accept all people. When he was seven his best friend was a black boy, and he came over to our house, just like any other kid."

"When I was a kid, my church choir traveled to D.C. I roomed with the only black girl in the group. We got along great!"

I watched the two black women—one a participant, one a group leader—to see if I could read judgment in their eyes. I couldn't. Nonetheless, I felt superior to the other participants, who didn't seem to hear how clueless they were.

After the last testimony of color-blindness, the lone black participant stood. "If y'all have such great times with black folk, why do we have so many problems?"

The room fell silent.

For the final leg of the Sacred Conversation on Race, I was paired with the black woman who assisted the group leader. We were to describe our first experience with race—the first time we became viscerally conscious of skin color.

I told her about the young girl in Forest Park. I didn't try to make it a fairy tale—two girls alike except for skin color. I knew that would be transparently false. I was acutely conscious of how the other white people sounded and was determined to go one better.

"I feel like I should apologize for being white," I said. The woman looked at me, puzzled. "I'm embarrassed about the things people have said," I explained.

"Don't be," she said. "None of us has it all figured out."

I immediately felt embarrassed for being embarrassed. I couldn't seem to get it right.

We exchanged our stories. She became aware of racial differences as a second-grader in an integrated school. I spoke of the tension in my family, about the split between my parents with respect to race, about my fear of drawing attention to what I saw outside the car window. Relating the story gave me the feeling of superiority I sought: I'm not like the clueless white people in this room. I come from a more complex, enlightened experience.

But I didn't tell the whole truth. I didn't tell the black woman I felt cheated and cheapened when I saw my dress on a Negro girl.

After that Easter Sunday I pushed the dress to the back of the closet. If I caught a glimpse of it, I fought the shame of having worn what I considered Negro clothes. Later, I fought the shame I felt for feeling shame. The latter struggle led to a revised memory of that Easter Sunday, one in which I focused on the wonder of my similarity with the girl who lived across a racial divide. For years I drew on a lazy, revisionist history, a convenience I tapped to make peace with an imperfect past.

The church gathering was two years ago. I wish I could go back and say what really happened the first time I became aware of the differences in the races: At eight years of age I'd absorbed the complexities of the racial divide in our country. I felt the fear, shame, and anger of this divide. And, despite a lifetime of effort to balance these irrational feelings with studied reason, I couldn't tell the truth during a Sacred Conversation on Race.

WINTER
Fabrice Poussin
photography
17x10

LOVESONG FOR THE MOON JELLYFISH

Laura Fairgrieve

"Where there is matter, there is geometry." —Johannes Kepler

I see your zooplankton, I raise you
the gummy core of a mollusk, this slippery
disk of rotifer and its gaping mouth
and two kicking toes (they know they will
soon be swallowed,
tied into tentacle and mucus twine
swilled among the dissolving fish eggs
that wait inside of you).

I see your limbs like wind chimes
in the water
hunting spears ready to drift
swift and sinister
and I raise you a Kreisel tank (watch
the water spin perfect circles
like the ones that bleed into the
water scrim above your limpid head
in your dreams).

I see your appendages sliced
and severed, one at a time

I see you rearranging,
organizing yourself into perfect lines
scrabbling together a new symmetry
where the old has been cut off
I see you smaller and surviving
and I raise you the ten days it took
to design your new lunar body
I raise you the scar that cannot
cling to your cloudy skin.

MOTHING

Laura Fairgrieve

I dreamed I was flat on my back in a crib—
there were moths sleeping underneath my skin
moldy wings rose to net up my hair
with snuffled sounds that nosed at my skin
rubbed behind my ear
and asked to be scrubbed clean of any grey.

My mobile looked like a crooked spider
and the cracks in the walls spun
a map of sketch marks I would later trace
the light that leaked through
my skull's fontanelle
beckoned the night time lepidoptera
out from inside the walls, the underside
of the kitchen table where the gum stuck,
and the corridors of my muscles and bones
(they love the dip of my clavicle)
where they weave their nests of wool
and gaseous starlight.

When I was older, I watched my brother crush them
with the flat of his shoe, the nub of his knuckle
I felt guts on my tongue and wings in my teeth

I watched them in the summertime
incinerated by the lick of a candle
zapped by the white hot planet of a light bulb
they couldn't stay away from.

They always flew too close to the airborne
fists of my brother's best friends,
they landed on the brims of baseball hats
they crowded the glow of freshly lit cigarettes
so they were swatted, smashed, smote,
they were scorched into crumpled
wrappers of dust.

Those stupid sun sluts
torn apart by transverse orientation
by their need to travel in straight lines
to follow the celestial bodies that bob above
those grey witches that used death machines
as their compass, and tried to make their homes
near bodies that smirked at murder, ignited lighters
to twirl and taunt them with
until their graphite bodies were nothing but ashes.
They never knew what was good for them.

BELGER
Katheryn Long
photography
7x5

SMOKE

Savannah Brooks

"Oh, shit, sorry." I'd stepped out onto the roof with my eyes on my book and had almost missed the guy on the ledge completely. His shadow swallowed up my feet.

He turned to look at me. The cloud directly behind his head made it look like he was wearing a crown.

"Just came up for some sun." I waved my book like it held an explanation. "But I'll uh, I'll go then."

I had almost made it back to the stairwell when he spoke. "You're just going to leave a man on the ledge like that?"

I shrugged. The sin of intrusion, beaten into me over time, eclipsed moral reasoning. "I can stay if you'd like company for your," I gestured, an empty palm to the surrounding skyline, "activities."

He swooped one leg down into the open air, making me feel a bit nauseated. "The more the merrier."

I walked up next to him and reached down into my purse. "Want a smoke?"

"Menthols?"

"Reds."

The exchange seemed innocuous enough, but hours later there we were, our heels bouncing off the side of the apartment building, daring our legs to stretch out just a little further into the nothingness.

"You know the end of *Brave New World*?" he asked. I nodded. "That's all I could think of." His eyes were staring past the skyline, past the edge of the world. "The way her feet just turned like that. I couldn't stop staring at her feet. Her fucking feet. Didn't even occur to me to try and get her down."

"My dad sold my bed for coke money," I said. He nodded, blowing smoke out of the side of his mouth. It was a logical enough response.

"Shit's fucked up."

We each took a drag, exhaling together, our smoke touching, briefly, then dissipating.

"Why'd she do it?" I asked.

He leaned back. The last of the sun lingered on him for just a moment longer. "I ask myself that every day." A pause. "It wasn't as if my dad were some bastard. It wasn't the usual shit. I don't know. I guess she was just broken somewhere inside. Something that couldn't be fixed." He shrugged. "Why'd your dad do it?"

"What, sell my bed?"

"All of it."

"He was some bastard."

He nodded again. The darkness was an ocean between the city street and us. He lit another cigarette.

"She had this pillow, you know the stitched ones you see, and it had that Dickinson quote, 'Hope is the thing with feathers.' It was damn uncomfortable, but it was always on her bed." He paused, inhaling, the end of his cigarette a tracer in the night. "I like to think wherever she is she found those feathers. That hope."

The wind had taken the place of the sun, flattening itself against the side of the building and catching my hair in the upswing. My toes felt vulnerable, having all that air slip around them. "What do you believe?"

"Don't know enough to believe."

"Fair enough," I said, stubbing out my spent cigarette.

"What about you?" He asked it sideways, teeth clamped against the cig in his mouth. His hands fumbled with the pack.

Years of burnt spoons and smashed beer bottles accumulated in a shrug. "I hope there's a hell."

He grabbed another cigarette and held the tip against his own, inhaling to light it for me. I placed it between my lips. "Actually, no. I don't. I hope it just ends. I hope he's just gone."

He nodded. Another gust of wind buffeted against us, and I turned my face into it, absorbing the smell of hot tar pounded down by thousands of feet.

"Guess we'll know when we know."

"Guess so."

We sat and watched the windows flicker to life, the wind humming through the dark, taking the place of silence. I reached for the packet of cigarettes, but it was empty.

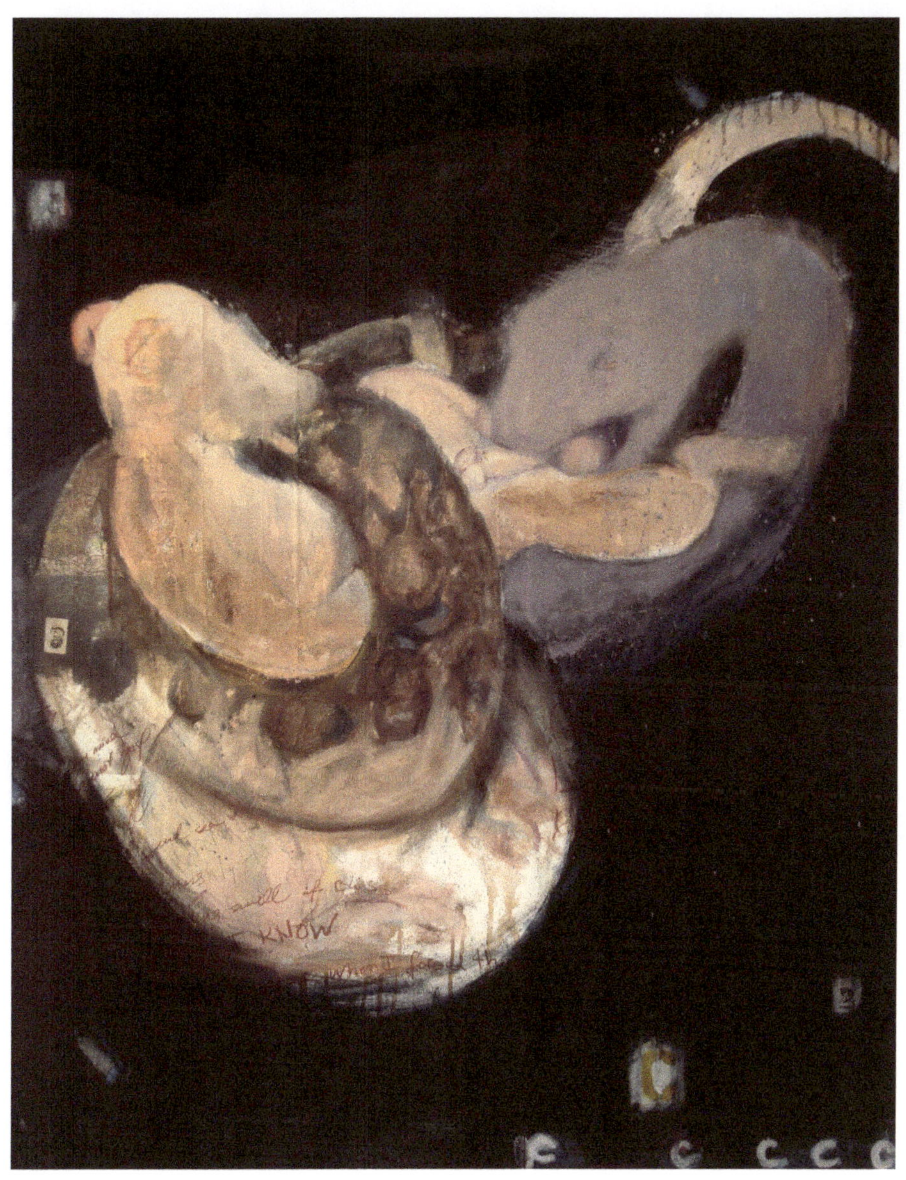

WEASEL WITH SERPENT UNDER APULEIUS'S TABLE
Stephen Linsteadt
oil and mixed media on canvas
36x48

PARADISE LOST

K.C. Bryce Fitzgerald

Jesus on the freeway saw a
billboard of himself; blond hair
and robes and praying for a
dollar; Jesus laughed and was
beheaded by a car
nobody stopped except a kid
in an Eldorado; he took a Jesus
selfie and drove off into the
billboard, too busy sharing
to care about the road or
himself, probably
the cops showed up and accidentally
shot someone
immigrant, perhaps, but does
it really matter
they towed the car and left the
billboard, laughing
down the road, smoke rose
but not from what
had happened.

BLUE CRABS

Deborah Phelps

We're all here on a summer afternoon. My mother lines the dining table with the *Evening Sun* and *Maryland Gazette,* then my father shakes the steamed crabs from a paper sack as we take up arms: wooden hammers and dinner knives to rip through carapaces and smash claw-joints. As the debris begins to grow taller than the piled crabs, we grow efficiently silent but for the cracking of back fin cartilage to gouge out the succulent lumps, crushing the claws for their darker, sweeter meat. We gather like this often in summer, when blue crabs are local to Baltimore. There's me, my near-Irish twin brother, my twelve-years-younger brother, two sisters-in-law, two grandsons, Mom and Dad. Mom the only adult without a beer in front of her. We are still pulling crab after crab from the tangle when abruptly my mother pushes back from the table: "Enough." We look up, startled. The crabs are excellent: heavy and still hot. Only a few times have I known her to leave the table first. Once (a family legend), our Thanksgiving bird had somehow spoiled before roasting back when we were a beginner family of four. And then there was her instinctive propriety, born of the post-World War II rationing burned in her brain from childhood in a house of eight. But today there is plenty. Today we are a model of the kind of family togetherness reflected in the Norman Rockwell prints she hung everywhere, as if to attract their wholesomeness. For decades "Freedom from Want" oversaw our dwindling attendance at table. But today we are all here, a happy family. Until she leaves. As she rose to wash the Old Bay muck from her hands I saw her press a paper towel-clad knuckle into her midriff even then malignant. Though her chin dipped I glimpsed the wince too soon a grimace, and herself all stilled.

DEALER

Seth Jani

My friend said he came across many miles.
The sea was wild in his voice.
"In everything," he said
"There is a restless element,
A longing that could crack the earth."

The hard egg of his body
Was full of ruptured light,
Full of savage, untamable lives,
And I too wanted to become
Bird-like and pure.

I followed him through every open window,
Under every bandage of the earth.
He said, "Only in the bowels
May you learn to sing,
All music is made of fire."

We sang, and the thirst between
Us grew,
The darkness keeled overhead.
From our deep, subterranean sorrows
Stars ascended through the night.

They too burned in the heavenly apparatus.
Somewhere between the cake
Of ash and reason
We tasted absolutes.
Pure grief and all its

Sister joys.
Longing like the taste
Of wild birds.
Elation, like one bit morsel
Of wind.

From him we learned to cut and measure
All the apocryphal fruits of man.

YAMDOOT
Stephen Linsteadt
ink on paper
20x31

IF PEOPLE WERE RAIN...

Ariel Alexia Sullivan

My high school did not ban books; they were more evolved than that. Instead, they had an unofficial list of undesirables. They couldn't tell the students not to bring these books to school, but that didn't mean they had to put them on the already scant wooden shelves. There was an unspoken rule in the library when it came to the Crutchers and the Kerouacs: Request all you want—you'll never find that trash in here.

I was fifteen years old when John Green's debut novel, *Looking for Alaska,* was published, and sixteen when it received the Michael L. Printz Award and suddenly began showing up by the dozens at every bookstore, covers all darkness and smoke on noisy cardboard displays. A few months into my junior year, I had fallen into a harrowing cycle of depression → loss of focus → failing classes → depression over failing classes, and I was too preoccupied to keep up with popular books (which, considering this was also the Dawn of Stephenie Meyer, probably benefited me in a lot of ways as well).

Tuesdays were my favorite days because the library stayed open until 5 o'clock, but most of the other students cleared out by 3:30 and the building was deserted save for the two older women who toiled away behind the counters, dabbing at their noses with balled up tissues and shuffling papers around on their desks. I came in with my shoulders slumped and my chin down, the default posture of a D-average student, but brightened slightly as the scent of ink and dust tickled my nose. I slid my bag off of my shoulder and dropped it unceremoniously onto one of the tables, and I felt like I was shedding the grime of failure and trading it in for something better—something purer—a book. I began wandering among the stacks, dragging my fingers over the cracked and faded spines, scanning them as I passed but finding nothing new. Back to an old preference, then. I located the library's only copy of *The Catcher in the Rye,* small enough that it almost fit in the palm of my hand, and so rough and worn from being hidden behind other books that the pages were barely holding together. I handled it carefully, granting it the same gentleness that I used when holding my newborn baby niece. I carried it back to my table and sat down, hunching over to cocoon myself in my own little world.

"You've read that one before, right?" I'd been following Holden around New York for at least an hour when Diane, the head librarian, appeared at the end of my table with a kind smile and her ever-present tissue.

I pressed my index finger against the last word I'd read before turning my attention to her, trying to return her smile with a watery imitation. "Only a couple dozen times."

"You know, most people find this book irritating," she noted, dabbing at her nose and craning her neck to skim the page I was on. "Holden is self-involved, dithery, anti-social; he's not exactly the kind of hero most people root for."

"That's why I like him. He's flawed. People are flawed." I wasn't used to talking so much, and it made me uncomfortable when I said more than a few words to any one person, so I ducked my head and turned my eyes back to the book. In my periphery, I saw Diane studying me for a moment before stepping back and disappearing into the small office behind the counter. A few minutes later, she gently set a book down on the table and slid it over to me, smile still in place but now a little nervous, like she was up to something devious.

When I gave her a curious look, she told me, "I read this last summer; I think you'll really enjoy it. Just..." She hesitated, chewing on her bottom lip and looking over her shoulder, "Tell people that you brought it from home, if they ask."

I nodded and reached out, pulling the book closer and studying the cover. It was black, with a puff of smoke rising from the bottom and three simple words printed in white. *Looking for Alaska*. I flipped open the cover and read the summary, and then closed it and slipped it into my bag, murmuring a quick "thanks" before picking back up with Holden. I didn't give Diane's book another thought until a few days later, when the bottom seam of my pack split and all the contents—the textbooks, the crumpled blank assignments, the unbottled aspirins—came spilling out onto the sidewalk between Buildings C and E. I felt tears stinging my eyes as helplessness overwhelmed me, and

I could feel myself shutting down. I decided to take this event as a sign that today would, in fact, not be my day, so I gathered what books I could carry and locked myself in one of the stalls in the science building bathroom. I had three hours to kill, sitting on the cold tile with my back against the door and my heels propped up on the stained porcelain, and not a lot of options. So I read.

And read, and read. And when the final bell rang, giving me the okay to emerge from my hiding place, I went home and read some more.

It was about depression. It was about fun and friendship, and troubles without resolution, and learning and trying to find your place in the world, and it was also, largely, about death. I read for hours on end, until my finger slid beneath the last line of the last page. "I don't know where there is," it read, "but I believe it's somewhere, and I hope it's beautiful." I carefully lowered the back cover and held the book close to my chest, the way I did only after finishing ones I really loved, trying to soak the ink into my skin and carry it with me always.

The next day, I returned the book to Diane. I thanked her, not just for the book, but for seeing what I was going through. I told her that *Looking for Alaska* made me feel just a little less alone, a little less strange, a little less despondent. "But it was kind of risky, wasn't it?" I asked her as we walked together to the door of the closing library. "It's a really depressing book; I could have just as easily interpreted it in a bad way."

She gave her nose a little dab and looked at me over her glasses, epitomizing the idea of a wise librarian, and said, "You're a smart girl—I knew you'd be able to tell. It's not a book about dying, Ariel; it's a book about continuing to live."

GARDEN DRAGON
Kevin Zepper
photography
15x12

MISFITS

Barbara Brady

Leonard picked at a scab on his forearm. He wished the sword tattoo he'd whittled with a matchstick and filled with ink hadn't come out blurry. He wiped a smudge of blood on his jeans.

"The Woodruff family looks forward to meeting you," Mrs. Evans the social worker said to Leonard. "I think you'll like living in the country."

A sneer crossed Leonard's thin lips. "Yeah, they'll explode with happiness when I'm dumped on them," he muttered in a barely audible voice. He leaned his head against the cool window of the car, closed his eyes and recalled the last foster family. He'd run away after four days. Cripes, he thought, I can beat that record.

Mrs. Evans left the highway and steered down a gravel road. She stopped the car in front of a farmhouse with peeling paint that looked like it'd been plastered with chicken feathers. The yard had large patches of dirt where grass should have been.

A barking dog with three scrawny legs lurched toward the car. A stubby appendage hung midair. Drool dripped from the dog's mouth and its tongue drooped like a black snake. "Get lost you stupid dog," Leonard hollered. "You've probably got rabies."

A screen door banged open and a skinny kid darted out. He had a crooked grin and bulgy eyes magnified behind thick glasses. Good gawd, thought Leonard, someone must have scrounged the city dump to find that ugly runt. The kid yanked open the car door and stuck his revolting face next to Leonard's. "Hi ya. I'm Michael. This is Pooch." He stooped down and hugged the deformed dog. "His leg got cut off in a mower."

"Yeah, well I'm the boogie man so shove off kid," Leonard snarled as he grabbed his duffel bag from the back seat. He opened the car door and nudged the dog and Michael aside. He glared at Mrs. Evans. "Let's get this over with."

"Remember, the Woodruffs are good people. Please give this your best try. Okay?"

Leonard grunted and made an obscene gesture behind her back. Inside, his latest foster parents greeted him. The woman wore jeans and a pink sweatshirt with a red heart stitched on the front. Bib overalls covered the man's lanky frame and hairy arms dangled by his sides. Holy shit, thought Leonard, these people are ancient. At least no one hugged him. Bogus touchy-feely stuff gave him the creeps.

In the living room Leonard flopped in a rocking chair so the weasel-faced kid wouldn't squeeze next to him. Michael and the crippled dog sprawled on the floor next to a fireplace.

"We're glad you made it okay on the back roads without getting lost," Mr. Woodruff said to Mrs. Evans. "I hope you'll stay for dinner."

"No thanks. I want to get home before dark." She turned to Leonard. "You have my phone number. If you have concerns, call me."

Leonard heard gravel crunch as Mrs. Evans drove away leaving him marooned in the boondocks—at least until he devised an escape plan.

"So what would you like us to call you?" asked Mrs. Woodruff.

"Huh? What?" Leonard ran his fingers through his dark hair and pulled some strands over pimples dotting his forehead.

"Do you have a nickname?" This came from Mr. Woodruff. "I'm Adam but everyone calls me Woody. Most people call my wife Nana."

Leonard hated his stuffy name. And being called Lenny made him want to puke. A social worker said he had his father's name. Why would he want to be named for a guy who didn't care diddly-squat if he even existed?

"You have a good strong name," volunteered Woody. "There was a famous boxer, Sugar Ray Leonard. And the King of Cowboys, Roy Rogers—his name was Leonard."

Leonard raised his eyebrows. "Uh, well maybe calling me Len will be okay."

"Len it is," Mrs. Woodruff said. The woman's wide smile reminded Len of someone. Yeah, that broad in the movies, Julia Roberts maybe, only fifty times older.

Woody heaved his rangy body from the sofa. He stopped in the foyer and hoisted Len's duffel bag on his shoulder. "Let's get you settled while Nana finishes dinner." Len followed Woody and Michael upstairs.

"For now you will bunk with Michael until I finish work on your room," explained Woody. "I'm doing it myself. Maybe you can help me pound a few nails." Before Len could grumble about having to work for his food, Woody motioned toward a tall chest of drawers. "You can stow your things here. Michael will help while Nana and I get dinner on the table." He left the two boys alone.

"So pee-wee, what do you really call those old geezers?"

"Woody and Nana, like he said."

"Christ Almighty! Don't they make you call them Mr. and Mrs. something?"

"No. I call them Woody and Nana." Michael scrunched his face and his lower lip trembled.

"What the hell's bugging you?"

"I…I…I'm sad when you talk like that. Nana says Jesus Christ is a beautiful name and shouldn't be used in bad ways."

"Look pipsqueak, I'll say whatever the heck I want." He paused. "Just don't cry, okay? I've heard enough blubbering at the shelter to last a lifetime." He didn't bother to unpack and headed to the kitchen letting the aroma of food cooking lead the way. The foster parents stood by the sink. Woody leaned close to his wife. Len overheard him ask, "Do you think the new boy likes us? Are we doing the right thing by him?"

Before she could answer Michael bounded into the room and interrupted their conversation. That settles it, Leonard thought. I'm toast. It won't take long for them to catch on to their mistake. The sooner I'm out of this dump the better.

The round table in the kitchen faced a bay window. The bright tablecloth made Len think of a big orange. Len noticed the heavy silverware. He should load up on the stuff before running away. It might bring some big bucks when he hawked it. A plan formed in head. He'd grab some loot tonight and take off. Maybe head for Florida. He'd heard Florida had nice beaches.

"Go ahead and be seated. The food will be on the table in a jiffy," Woody announced. He wore a green apron with a rooster on the pocket.

"Does the old guy cook?" Len whispered to Michael.

"Nana has been sick so Woody helps her a lot."

"Yeah, she looks kinda weak. That's what old age does."

They gathered around the table. Len inhaled the scent of fried meat, apples and cinnamon and eyed the heaping bowls of food. His empty stomach growled. He hadn't seen such a feast since being dragged to a Thanksgiving dinner at some church. He knew from experience foster parents liked to impress a kid on the first night in case a social worker hung around so he'd load up while he could.

Everyone passed food at once. Len piled a blob of mashed potatoes on his plate, smashed a hole in the center, and dumped in gravy until it overflowed like a volcano. He forked a chunk of meat, took some corn, but skipped the creamed peas. He scooped a spoon of banana Jell-O on his plate. A wiggly piece hung over the edge and dropped on the tablecloth, making a red stain. No one yelled so he crammed food into his mouth, barely chewing.

"Do you want to hear a riddle?" Michael asked with his mouth full of mashed potatoes. "How do fireflies start a race?" he asked. The adults smiled and shrugged. "Ready, get set, glow!" blurted Michael like he'd told the world's cleverest riddle. Without pausing he continued. "What always comes at the end of Thanksgiving?" No one guessed. "The letter G," he announced.

Michael gulped some milk leaving a creamy mustache on his upper lip. "Here's another one. What has legs but can't walk?" Everyone but Len shook their heads. "A chair!" beamed Michael.

The Woodruffs grinned like happy jack-o-lanterns. "That's great," said Woody. Nana chuckled and said she'd never heard such clever riddles.

Jeez, the kid thinks he's another Jay Leno, Len thought. A tinge of jealousy swept through him.

Nana served apple cobbler for dessert. When everyone's plate was empty she said, "Tonight you get to be treated as a guest, Len. Woody and I will do the dishes." She flashed her movie star smile. "After tonight you will have your turn."

"Hey, twerp," said Len. "Come here." Michael followed him outside and they sat on a squeaky porch swing. "What's the deal with the woman? You said she's sick?"

"Yeah. Nana had cancer so she takes medicine. Once her hair all fell out. Woody said she'll be okay and won't die."

"Holy shit! I mean, heck, that's a bummer. How come they had all that food tonight?"

"What do you mean?" Thick glasses magnified Michael's eyes and made them look like shiny marbles.

"What do you usually eat? Regular like?"

Michael shrugged. "Good food. Nana and Woody like to cook. Sometimes I help bake cookies."

"No gummy oatmeal?"

"Nah. Usually bacon and eggs for breakfast. Maybe cold cereal. I like Froot Loops best. Do you like Froot Loops?"

"They're okay." Len didn't admit he'd never had Froot Loops.

Woody and Nana came into bedroom later to say goodnight. Nana sat on the edge of Len's bed and smoothed the covers. "We're glad you are here, Len." She grasped his hand in hers. Her hands felt silky and she smelled like vanilla frosting. He watched the foster parents leave the room clinging together like two teenagers.

Len lay awake and tried to plan his escape. But Woody's words kept stirring around in his head and confused him. What the heck did Woody mean—would I like them? Since when did anyone care if he liked them? His feelings got all jumbled so he knew he'd better stick to his plan and get out now. Michael made soft snoring sounds so Len hurriedly dressed, grabbed his duffel bag, and crept downstairs. He remembered to stop in the kitchen to snatch some silverware. Thoughts of dinner made him want to grab a hunk of apple cobbler but instead he hunted around until he found the silverware drawer and quickly stuffed a handful of spoons in his duffel bag. A serving spoon slipped from his hand and made a clunk. Fearful the Woodruffs might wake, he closed the duffel bag and sneaked out the door.

A moonlit sky helped him see in the darkness. Dragging his heavy duffel bag by the cord Len hustled down the driveway. Before he reached the main road he felt a tug on the bag, turned and saw the gimpy dog. "Go back, get outta here," Len scolded and quickened his pace. The persistent mutt nipped at Len's heels and pranced around trying to play. "Shoo. Go home." He kicked at the dog but the pup merely squealed and flopped down at Len's feet. Len couldn't resist petting his furry head. The dog rolled on his back and licked Len's hand. The sloppy tongue felt warm and comforting. Len plunked himself on the gravel driveway and gathered the dog in his arms. He held the deformed dog close to his chest and let him lick the tears from his face.

TRIANGLE WALKS
Katheryn Long
photography
7x5

THE MAN IN THE HAT

Suzanne O'Connell

I was half asleep when the phone rang.
She apologized for waking me
but I didn't mind.
She paid me double time at night
and there were no guns involved.
Her husband was missing again.
This time his note read,
"To Pants Unknown," she said.
I had to hold back a laugh.

When Mrs. Ernst hired me,
I wondered whether her husband
was running away from something
or toward something better.
"Is there any reason to think Mr. Ernst
is unhappy at home?" I asked.
She assured me he loved her very much,
gave me some background:
architect, designer of downtown buildings,
sixty-one years old, thin,
always wore a suit and tie—even when he
wandered—and he never left home without his hat.
Since he retired, he seemed angry and confused.

It would be easier to find him this time.
Mrs. Ernst had bought a GPS bracelet
that blinked his location.
Once in the vicinity,
his natty clothing would
make him easy to spot.

The tracking device led me to
the L.A. River near Chinatown.
Over the rise I saw a sign
advertising HOP SUEY—
the neon C trembled in the darkness.

Trees outlined the path,
branches reached out their leafy arms.
I could hear the trickle of water.
I saw two ducks pecking for bugs,
but I didn't see him.

The moon was misty and dim.

As I drew near the riverbank,
I saw a hat floating on the surface.
A green band of light flickered under the water,
and my tracking device pulsed Arrived.

RES IPSA LOQUITUR

Kendra Tanacea

An inference arises: Assume the existence
of a presumed fact unless there's contrary evidence.

So, when an oak door falls off its hinges, crushes the skull
of a young girl, you say, *The thing speaks for itself.*

Something went terribly wrong, even if you can't exactly
say. Bones now powdered, does she rise like incense

smoky, sweet? Somewhere, she waits, wonders if
she'll ever recognize her family without their bodies.

When we buried our dog, I prayed. But our priest said,
Dogs don't go to heaven, just decompose. So, *res ipsa loquitur.*

Dust to dust. Scientists argue our minds are electrical.
When the plug is pulled, lights out. But just before final darkness,

there's a crackle, a spark from the sudden yank.
The white light? The sleight of hand called heaven?

Or will I return? A dog? A cow? Better wisteria.
The thing speaks for itself, harbinger of spring.

I NEVER WORE A TRAINING BRA

Donna Emerson

In seventh grade, my mother announced it was time to leave my undershirt.
I said *No*. Loved my quilted white, soft against me.
It fit snugly under my whole slip. Loved the "Carter's" tag in the back,
one of the few well-made pieces of clothing I owned.
My breasts did not look like the ones in the Woman book, so what's the rush?
They looked to me like they always had. Like golden raisins.

Mother insisted at Christmas we shop. We went to Dunham's in Trenton.
I tried to hide behind the curtain as the elderly woman handed thirty-two AA's to us. No one
used the words *training bra*. They hadn't been invented yet. What do they train?

In Dunham's corner room with the gray curtain, I didn't feel proud.
Or excited, though Mom exclaimed, *You're growing up!*
My stomach felt like something was being taken from me.

ON BEING LATE

Barry Zabell

"A dog ate my homeboy."

Mrs. Marquetta looked at me as if I'd just pissed myself. Revulsion and disbelief battled to own her expression. As she stood over me, her eyes found my cell phone on my desk. A few weeks before I'd taken a photograph of her from behind and was using the picture as wallpaper. A smile creased the tips of her mouth when she recognized herself, momentarily forgetting that I did not complete the class assignment. Deborah Thomson giggled and kicked my seat with the points of her shoes.

Mrs. Marquetta lingered, her eyes darting back and forth from my phone to my face. "Explain yourself," she demanded.

Was she more concerned about my delinquent work or my appreciation of her world-class bottom? I decided to address the easier subject. "I was all set to get it done last night when my doorbell rang." I was talking to her back as she sashayed back to her desk. Was she walking deliberately slow? She folded her arms over her chest and stared me down for more information. A raised eyebrow signaled me to continue. "Albert's mother, she came over all upset, crying like a waterfall. At first I couldn't understand what she was trying to say. Most of the time she was just hacking and sniffling."

Ronnie Gold covered his mouth with his fist and said something through a cough so Mrs. Marquetta couldn't make it out. However, she understood when I flashed him the finger.

"I think you've wasted enough of our time today," she said, opening a small brown notebook to record how I failed her that morning. I'm sure the page with my name on it had more entries than anyone else's. This time, and for the first time, I objected to the notation.

"Albert, Albert Cortez, he got bit by a pit bull, got bit real bad."

All of the faces in the room turned in my direction. Mrs. Marquetta stopped writing and placed the book down. She walked around the desk and leaned her beautiful derriere against it. I imagined the lip of the desk putting a crease in the image on my phone. Her arms covered her breasts again.

"I went to the hospital to see how he was doing. It was late, after visiting hours, but they let me see him anyway, probably because they don't expect him to make it."

Someone behind me gasped. Ellen Tavares put her head into her hands and started to sob.

"His face, everything was covered by bandages. Blood was still coming through. There were all kinds of wires and tubes, monitors flashing and beeping. Little bags were hanging from the bed. I think they were for him to..."

"We don't need all the gory details," Mrs. Marquetta snapped. She picked up a pencil and pulled it across something she had written in the book. "I'm sure all of us will pray that Albert will be all right." She scanned the room for affirming nods. "In the meantime, be sure to bring in your story tomorrow."

I missed school the next day and the day after that so I could go to Albert's funeral. It wasn't big or fancy, a dozen people from the neighborhood and his mother and sister. When I finally returned to class I left this story on Mrs. Marquetta's desk. I guess she won't mind too much that it's late.

SMILE WHILE YOU STILL CAN

Jason Hanna

Holga 120 film

8x10

THE PROPOSITION

Peter Grimes

I'm her diminutive husband.
She carries me in socket
wrench cases, sometimes, in a head-
lock, according to mood.

I'm the rooster gone mad
in the barn, all blade and sickles
with buttercup comb. Gouged walls
and dander are my tokens.

I'm the stranger you passed,
a weak-impressioning sack
of flesh. You smile at me inwardly,
my scarf reminding you of cake.

I'm your anatomy exam,
hired to render the body
strange. I map the male
uterus, your shrinking pinkie.

I'm your ugly sweater contest,
knit for you by gnarls of dead
women. Which one led the quietest life,

froze the mole on your back, wept?

I'm your bedroom door.
I creak when you leave me, guarding
your talc. I sense your moods
with my blond, flat wood.

I'm your Kindergarten cranium,
your kicked-at ball, your menstrual
detour, a filigree of faith,
the driftwood drying inside you.

Contributors

Barbara Brady lives in Topeka, Kansas, with her husband of 61 years. Auditing classes on prose and poetry at Washburn University inspired her interest in writing. She is member of the Kansas Authors Club.

Savannah Brooks is a graduate student pursuing her M.F.A. in creative writing at Hamline University in Saint Paul, Minnesota. She is the production editor of Hamline's graduate literary magazine, *rock, paper, scissors,* and the assistant fiction editor of Hamline's literary annual, the *Water~Stone Review.*

Newspapers and magazines have published some 1,600 articles under **Marty Carlock**'s byline. She is the author of two editions of *A Guide to Public Art in Greater Boston.* She writes for magazines, and reviews fiction and nonfiction for *The Internet Review of Books.*

Susana H. Case's newest book is *4 Rms w Vu* (Mayapple Press, 2014). Author of four full-length poetry collections and four chapbooks, including *The Scottish Café,* which was re-released in a Polish-English version, *Kawiarnia Szkocka,* by Opole University Press, she is a professor at the New York Institute of Technology.

Some of **Donna Emerson**'s publications include *CQ (California Quarterly), CALYX, The Chaffin, Dos Passos Review, Edison Literary Review, The Los Angeles Review, LUX, New Ohio Review, Paterson Literary Review, Passager, Praxis: Gender & Cultural Critiques, Quiddity, Sanskrit, Slipstream, Soundings East, The South Carolina Review,* and *Weber—The Contemporary West.*

Laura Fairgrieve received her M.F.A. from Adelphi University, where she currently teaches. Her work has appeared in *East Coast Ink, Words Dance Publishing,* and *Village of Crickets,* and is forthcoming in *The Bitchin' Kitsch.* She is a winner of the 2016 Poets & Writers Amy Award. She lives in Brooklyn.

Patricia Feeney's work has appeared in *The Lindenwood Review,* the anthology *Shifts* (MuseWrite Press, 2014), and *Bayou Magazine,* which published a Pushcart Prize nomination. Feeney teaches English in two St. Louis colleges and participates in Crooked Writers, a local writing workshop.

K.C. Bryce Fitzgerald was born in Los Angeles, where he has been writing since he was five years old. He was the featured poet in the *Burningword Literary Journal* for April 2015 and is currently publishing his debut novel, *The Lines of Union,* with Bookshop Santa Cruz. When not helming his local film production company, he is busy working on two books of poetry, short stories, countless film projects, and his second novel. He lives in Santa Cruz.

Corey Ginsberg's chapbook, *Bowling in the Bumper Lane,* is forthcoming from WordTech Press. Her nonfiction has been listed as a Notable in *The Best American Essays* in 2012 and 2014.

Peter Grimes is an assistant professor of English at Dickinson State University. His fiction has appeared in numerous journals, including *Narrative, Hayden's Ferry Review, Mississippi Review,* and *Sycamore Review.*

Maria Haag is a graphic artist by day and painter by night—and by early morning, and sometimes by lunch break—who lives in Arlington, Texas. She graduated with her B.F.A. in painting from Washburn University in 2014.

Jason Hanna has been trapped in Kansas all his life but plans to soon venture out to bigger and better places. He is double-majoring in creative writing and fine arts at Washburn University, and plans to apply to graduate programs thereafter. He awaits the new beginning where he will finally be able to narrow his focus towards his own visions and dreams.

Seth Jani lives in Seattle and is the founder of Seven CirclePress (www.sevencirclepress.com). His own work has been published widely in such places as the *Coe Review, The Hamilton Stone Review, Hawai`i Pacific Review, VAYAVYA, Gingerbread House, Gravel* and *Zetetic: A Record of Unusual Inquiry*. More about him and his work can be found at www.sethjani.com.

Stephen Linsteadt is a painter, poet, and writer. His recent poetry collection is titled *The Beauty of Curved Space* (Glass Lyre Press). His poetry is also published in *California Quarterly, Silver Birch Press, Synesthesia Literary Journal, Pirene's Fountain, The Poetry Box,* and others.

Katheryn Long is an art student at Washburn University and a Kansas native. She enjoys writing, photography, and digital art.

Jayne Marek's poems and photos have appeared in *New Mexico Review, Peacock Journal, Camas, Gravel, Blast Furnace, Sliver of Stone, Spillway, Flying Island, Tipton Poetry Journal,* and elsewhere. She is author of a chapbook and co-author of another poetry collection. Her work has twice been nominated for a Pushcart Prize.

Anna Maxymiw lives in Toronto. Her writing has been featured in such publications as *The Globe and Mail, The Walrus,* and *Hazlitt,* and has won a National Magazine Award.

Suzanne O'Connell's recently published work can be found in *Atlanta Review, The Louisville Review, Poet Lore, Pamplemousse,* and others. She was a Best Of The Net and Pushcart nominee in 2015. Her book of collected poems, *A Prayer For Torn Stocking,* was published in 2016.

Deborah Phelps teaches creative writing and British literature at Sam Houston State University. She has published a chapbook, *Deep East* (Small Poetry Press, selected by Stephen Dunn), and poetry in journals such as *Slipstream, Gulf Coast,* and *Southern Poetry Review.* She lives in Huntsville, Texas.

Jim Plath is an author of fiction and poetry. He holds a B.F.A. in creative writing from the University of Nebraska at Omaha. His work has appeared in a variety of publications, some of which are linked through his website www.jimplath.com.

Fabrice Poussin teaches French and English at Shorter University in Rome, Georgia. His work has appeared in *Kestrel, Symposium, The Chimes,* and more than a dozen other magazines. His photography has been published in *Front Porch Review, San Pedro River Review,* and more than sixty other publications.

Ina Roy-Faderman's work is found in *Punchnel's, Right Hand Pointing,* and *Danny Shot's Long Shot,* among others. She has an M.D. (Stanford) and Ph.D. (philosophy, U.C. Berkeley) and lives near San Francisco, where she writes, teaches bioethics, and edits for *Rivet Journal* and the forthcoming *56DaysofAugust* (Five Oaks Press).

Frank Rubino's poetry has been published in *The World, Little Light,* and *New Directions.* A former student of both Eileen Myles and Ted Berrigan, he has been performing his poetry since 1982, reading at St. Mark's Poetry Project, the Ear Inn, the Cornelia Street Cafe, the Nuyorican Poets Cafe, and numerous other locations in and around New York. He lives in New Jersey with his wife and four children.

Ariel Alexia Sullivan holds no degrees and has no publications to her name, though she did win a statewide writing award as a teenager that gave her a false sense of self that took years to shake off. She looks forward to being rejected by the Walt Whitman Award in April, and spends way too much time Facebooking about her cat.

Kendra Tanacea, an attorney, holds an M.F.A. in writing and literature from Bennington College. Her collection of poetry, *A Filament Burns in Blue Degrees,* was a semifinalist for the Washington Prize and a finalist for the Idaho Prize for Poetry, and will be published by Lost Horse Press in early 2017. Kendra's poems have appeared in *5AM, Rattle, Pearl,* and *Pebble Lake Review,* among others.

July Westhale is a poet and essayist living in Oakland, California. She is the author of the chapbook *The Cavalcade* (Finishing Line Press), and has poems in *Cimarron Review, cahoodaloodaling, burntdistrict,* and *Quarterly West,* among others. Her essays have appeared in *The Huffington Post, Autostraddle, The Establistment,* and elsewhere. She has been awarded grants and residencies from the Vermont Studio Center, the Sewanee Writers' Conference, Dickinson House, Tin House, and Bread Loaf.

Linda Wimberly is an artist, writer and musician from Marietta, Georgia. Her poetry has appeared in *Stone River Sky: An Anthology of Georgia Poems, Kalliope,* and others, and a short story appeared in *Cricket*. She is a self-taught abstract contemporary artist who works in acrylic, oil, and mixed media.

Barry Zabell's stories have recently appeared in *Dali's Lovechild, Mash Stories, Down in the Dirt,* and *Coup D'Etat,* Boston University's literary magazine. He is nearing completion of his first novel.

Kevin Zepper teaches at Minnesota State University Moorhead. He is part of a music/poetry duo called Lines&Notes. To date, he has published four chapbooks of poetry.

www.ingramcontent.com/pod-product-compliance
Lightning Source LLC
Chambersburg PA
CBHW061108100726
47911CB00012B/461